DC SUPER-PETS!™

Raintree is an imprint of Capstone Global Library Limited, a company incorporated in
England and Wales having its registered office at 264 Banbury Road, Oxford, OX2 7DY –
Registered company number: 6695582

www.raintree.co.uk
myorders@raintree.co.uk

STAR39901

ISBN 978 1 4747 4898 8
21 20 19 18 17
10 9 8 7 6 5 4 3 2 1

British Library Cataloguing in Publication Data
A full catalogue record for this book is available from
the British Library.

Designed by Bob Lentz

Printed and bound in China.

JUMPA!

The Origin of Wonder Woman's Kanga

by Steve Korté

illustrated by Art Baltazar

Wonder Woman created by William Moulton Marston

raintree

a Capstone company — publishers for children

EVERY SUPER HERO NEEDS A
SUPER-PET!

Even Wonder Woman!
In this origin story, discover
how Jumpa the Kanga
became the Amazon Princess'
loyal steed . . .

On a secret island lives a powerful group of women – the **AMAZONS!**

The Amazons call their home **Paradise Island.**

A wise queen called **Hippolyta** rules their kingdom.

No men or children live on the island.

But many **amazing animals** roam the rich forests.

During sporting contests, the Amazons
often ride on these **wild beasts!**

The Amazons enjoy riding one animal most of all – **KANGAS!**

These queen-size kangaroos are only found on Paradise Island.

Kangas stand much taller than kangaroos from Australia. They jump much farther too!

One day on Paradise Island, the smallest of all kangas is born.

"I will call her Jumpa," her mother says proudly.

Other kangas laugh. "That's a mighty big name for such a runt!"

At the same time, Hippolyta becomes a mother to the island's first child.

"I shall call you Diana," says the queen.

"The perfect name for a princess!" the other royals agree.

As Jumpa grows, she hopes to live up to her high-hopping name.

"Watch me!" Jumpa tells her friends.

BOINK. BOINK.

"Ha! You'll never be a big bouncer, Jumpa!" they tease.

As Diana grows, she wants to make a name for herself.

"One day, I'll be a champion athlete," she tells her mother.

"You are a princess," Hippolyta replies, "not a warrior."

To prove her mother wrong, Diana trains every day at the beach.

Then one day, a **harpy attacks!**

"CAW! CAW!" The monster carries the princess into the sky.

"Not so fast!" Diana shouts.

Diana punches the harpy with all her might. KA-POW!

The monster drops her in mid-air!

Suddenly, Jumpa bounds onto the beach and spots Diana in trouble.

"I must do something!" the young kanga tells herself.

In the face of danger, Jumpa leaps higher than ever before!

WHUMP!

Diana lands right on her back.

"You are my high-hopping hero!"
Diana says as they land.

Jumpa smiles. **"And you are my powerful princess!"** she thinks.

The new friends set out to show their talents to others.

Soon, Diana gets her chance.

The princess chooses to leave the island and face an evil enemy.

After proving she is ready, Diana becomes . . . **WONDER WOMAN!**

The warrior princess says goodbye to her mother and the other Amazons.

She hugs her favourite kanga, and a tear falls from Jumpa's eye.

"I'll be back soon," says Diana.

After defeating her enemy, Wonder Woman returns to Paradise Island.

The hero learns that the Amazons are planning a sporting contest.

She leaps onto Jumpa's back.

"Come on, old friend," Wonder Woman tells her. **"Everyone must see your high-hopping heroics!"**

Inside the arena, kangas jump high into the air. BOING! BOING!

The Amazons swing their golden lassos. FWOOSH! FWOOSH!

With Wonder Woman on her back,
Jumpa sails over the other kangas.

The super hero lassos eleven Amazons
and pulls them off their kangas.

"WOO-HOO!" the crowd cheers.

Just then, the Amazons' champion athlete appears.

"Mala!" Wonder Woman gasps.

Jumpa spots Mala's trusty steed. **"Show-off!"** she grumbles.

Mala quickly lassos Wonder Woman.

Mala's kanga charges at Jumpa!

Wonder Woman flexes her muscles.

SNAAAP! Mala's lasso breaks apart!

Then Jumpa stretches out her tail and trips Mala's kanga.

"Oof!" Mala and her steed hit the ground with a **THUD.**

Wonder Woman and Jumpa win the first contest!

The final contest is a **boxing match.**

Each Amazon grabs a wooden pole with a boxing glove at one end.

Mala and her kanga face directly towards Wonder Woman and Jumpa.

"Watch out, princess!" Mala shouts angrily.

"SNORT! SNORT!" Mala's kanga

huffs at Jumpa.

Jumpa and Mala's kanga leap towards each other.

Mala's boxing glove is aimed right at Wonder Woman's head!

"Oh no!" Jumpa thinks.

At the last second, the young kanga presses her tail against the ground.

THUMP!

The power of her legs and tail together send Jumpa soaring through the air!

BOOooOOiLLiiNNNNGGGg!!!

Jumpa hops higher than Mala's kanga!

Mala loses her balance and drops her boxing pole.

Mala's steed trips over the boxing pole, and the team crashes to the ground.

WHUMP!

"Congrats, Diana!" Queen Hippolyta says. **"You are the winner!"**

Then Hippolyta walks over to Jumpa.

"Because of her strength and skill, Jumpa will be Diana's official Super-Pet!" says the queen.

She places a tiara, a golden necklace and silver bracelets on the kanga.

"I am honoured," thinks Jumpa.

From that day forwards, the young kanga has Wonder Woman's back.

Whether facing a wicked cheetah or an evil giant, **Jumpa is there.**

Because no matter how brave or how bold . . .

EVERY SUPER HERO NEEDS A SUPER-PET!

JUMPA!

REAL NAME:
Jumpa

SPECIES:
Kanga

BIRTHPLACE:
Paradise Island

HEIGHT:
254 centimetres

WEIGHT:
127 kilograms

Super hero owner:
WONDER WOMAN

ROYAL TIARA
Jumpa's glittering gold tiara can also be used as a weapon. When facing a dangerous threat, Jumpa will throw the razor-sharp tiara at her foe.

SUPER HEARING

HANDY POUCH
When Jumpa sleeps, she stores her royal tiara, necklace and bracelets inside her pouch.

GOLDEN NECKLACE

SILVER BRACELETS

SUPER-STRONG TAIL
Years of training have strengthened Jumpa's legs and her powerful tail.

POWERFUL LEGS
Jumpa can hop up to six metres in the air.

HERO PET PALS!

LEEPA
Super hero owner:
WONDER GIRL

YOONI

Super hero owner:
CASSIE

MATILDA

Super hero owner:
CECELIA

STORM
Super hero owner:
AQUAMAN

COMET

Super hero owner:
SUPERGIRL

JEWELLION

Super hero owner:
AMETHYST

VILLAIN PET FOES!

CHAUNCEY
Super-villain owner:
CHEETAH

ADORA

Super-villain owner:
STAR SAPPHIRE

GRYLL
Super-villain owner:
CIRCE

COMO

Super-villain owner:
GORILLA GRODD

PATCHES

Super-villain owner:
GIGANTA

KANGA JOKES!

How do injured kangas get better?

They have a hop-eration!

What do you call a kanga's uniform?

A jumpsuit!

What is a kanga's favourite type of music?

Hip-hop!

GLOSSARY!

Amazons group of female warriors who live on Paradise Island

arena large building that is used for sporting events

Hippolyta Queen of the Amazons and the mother of Wonder Woman

lasso length of rope with a large loop at one end that can be thrown over an animal to catch it

paradise place that is very beautiful

runt smallest animal in a group

tiara headpiece, usually worn by women

warrior someone who is experienced in fighting battles

READ THEM ALL!

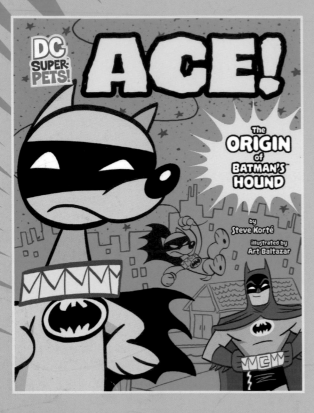

AUTHOR!

Steve Korté is the author of many books for children and young adults. He worked at DC Comics for many years, editing more than 600 books about Superman, Batman, Wonder Woman and the other heroes and villains in the DC Universe. He lives in New York, USA, with his own super-cat, Duke.

ILLUSTRATOR!

Famous cartoonist Art Baltazar is the creative force behind *The New York Times* bestselling, Eisner Award-winning DC Comics' Tiny Titans; co-writer for Billy Batson and the Magic of Shazam, Young Justice, Green Lantern Animated (Comic); and artist/co-writer for the Tiny Titans/ Little Archie crossover, Superman Family Adventures, Super Powers and Itty Bitty Hellboy! Art is one of the founders of Aw Yeah Comics. He stays at home and draws comics and never has to leave the house! He lives with his lovely wife, Rose, sons Sonny and Gordon, and daughter Audrey. Visit him at www.artbaltazar.com